Corporate Fear in America

The Google Problem

By Robert George

The Google Problem

By Robert George

© Copyright 2018 by Robert George

Contact: robertgeorge124@outlook.com

Printed in the United States of America

ISBN-13: 978-1983917288 (CreateSpace-Assigned)
ISBN-10: 1983917281
BISAC: Business & Economics / Business Ethics

Table of Contents

Introduction

We've heard a lot about Google, Inc.; one of the largest and most powerful companies in the world. We've heard about its culture, its hiring practices, lawsuits and troubles with the government. Recently, the company has been scrutinized by the media over its firing of a young employee who had written a paper about its diversity policies. I did a Google search, so I could read the paper written by James Damore using the search term "Text of James Damore's Paper".

The paper is entitled "Google's Ideological Echo Chamber"; but it is not about that; it is about gender diversity at Google and how the liberal policies of the company have affected its hiring practices. The fact that the title does not reflect the actual subject of the paper is a clear indication that it is not intended to be an organized work of writing but a stream of consciousness rant that expresses opinion rather than reasoned thought or scientific research.

The idea of diversity in the workplace is essentially a collectivist notion; it holds that specific groups should be given hiring priority based upon their grievances. Although collectivism is a broad philosophical concept that goes back centuries, today's variation of it goes back to the early diversity movement from the 1980s and '90s when American companies created "Diversity Programs" to address the issue of whether they were engaged in bias toward certain groups in their hiring and employment practices. But it also goes back to earlier government programs such as the Equal Employment Opportunity Commission in which certain individuals were designated as members of "protected groups". Before that, Affirmative Action required corporations to target for employment certain protected minorities to "level" the playing field racially and ethnically.

Specifically, as it regards gender differences, diversity practices hold that men are historically biased against women. To complement this view, it also holds that capitalist corporations, most often led by men, are naturally sexist and focused on ensuring that women take a secondary role in the business.

Few people questioned the assumption that white people are racists because they were supposedly descendants of the conquering hoards who once forcibly displaced "natives" before founding this nation. Few companies defended themselves or pointed out that they had been engaging in "merit-based" hiring for decades. Most critics assumed that "capitalist" corporations, because they were "for-profit", must be racist and sexist. Most ignored the fact that capitalist organizations, in order to compete, must be "rational" in their hiring practices and promote people according to their abilities rather than skin color. Few people even noticed that most corporations were looking for the best people regardless of color. The mere assumption that they were racist was all the left needed to steal the issue and make fighting racism into an anti-capitalist campaign.

This booklet will analyze the concept of diversity politics in corporate America. As a young executive, working for a major corporation, I observed the issue of diversity as it played out during the '70s and into the new century. I'd like to offer this perspective to help us understand what I have come to call Corporate Fear in America and how it has developed over those decades.

Differences

The idea that "women" are a separate category of human being in the workplace is a false notion. Although, it is true that many men subconsciously hold this view, the idea that "women" are discriminated against in the work environment, despite their productive ability, is wrong. We can see this if take a different perspective on competence and look at the "individual".

When it comes to the so-called differences between men and women in the modern work place, there is no difference when it comes to intelligence, aptitude and mental acuity; the issues that matter when it comes to productivity. In fact, if there are any differences (generally), they are so minute that using them to distinguish men from women, and especially, using them to develop policy, is futile. These minute differences tell us nothing about individuals nor can they be used to create distinct groups of any kind.

For instance, one woman may be more intelligent than all the men she knows, but that has nothing to do with her being a woman. In fact, on the level of real world action, individual characteristics like intelligence range across both men and women to such an extent that we cannot conclude, generally, that men and women are different in terms of intelligence.

What distinguishes individuals on this level are their

choices, knowledge, personal attitudes and effort. Just as, generally, there is no difference between men of color, there are, generally, no significant differences between the sexes. One cannot take a so-called "scientific" study and credibly declare that women are, for instance, more caring than men. What does "more caring than men" mean and how does one measure that except through anecdotal thinking? Women go through childbirth and that means they must care more? That is pseudo-science. That is sexist.

The flaw in the thinking here is collectivism, not general differences between the sexes. A collective (or artificial grouping) would necessarily include people with all sorts of differences, and as such, it would include (and discriminate against) people within the group that do not contain those characteristics.

Regarding men and women, real differences among individuals start with the mind; volition, the choice to think; and then with the persistent application of choice by individuals living according to their individual levels of established knowledge.

In an environment where everyone is responsible for his or her own survival, as is the case today, what becomes important is the ability to survive and, today, this is a matter of applied intelligence. This means that companies cannot succeed unless they discriminate in favor of human choice (volition) aimed at excellence. This is not wrong; it is within the self-interest of the corporation to discriminate in this way. To succeed, it must have the best employees whose capabilities enable the successful accomplishment of the corporation's mission. It must hire individuals who possess those capabilities, or it must have a training system capable of producing those individuals.

Hiring practices that would create success in the knowledge industry, for instance, must focus on finding individuals who are able to exert diligence and competence in delivering their work products. These work products must benefit customers who are seeking usable knowledge. Any productive person offering such work products can succeed if he or she has the desire to succeed and chooses to acquire the best knowledge and ability possible. In the knowledge industry, it is about the mind, not the body.

In fact, some women today can do any job that any man can do and vice versa. In most cases, they can work at an equal level of competence, strength and ability. The key challenge for any such individual is not genetic differences but desire to be as productive as other humans regardless of their sex.

Collectivism, as part of a diversity policy, divides people into groups of disparate individuals. This leads to an ineffective policy for those individuals of ability who are not included within the desired groups. Collective divisions elevate many people who cannot perform certain jobs and the effort to have more women in certain positions does not ensure that all those women are capable. In effect, it asserts that ability is not important, but gender is.

When we elevate people to certain positions because we think they have been discriminated against, the result is exploitation of the able people who will have to "make up for" the work not accomplished by the less competent. This is discrimination against competent men and women in the name of equality (egalitarianism). The effort to level the playing field through intervention in the affairs of men becomes a coercive effort to exploit the best minds and force them to sacrifice for the sake of lesser minds. The result is that the company will suffer against competitors who find a way to reward merit first.

Superficial differences between individuals should never be the basis of corporate or government policies. Technocratic meddling is destructive and disruptive of good business practices. Such interferences are themselves discriminatory toward individuals seeking professional competence. Individual competence is the only meaningful standard for judging the quality of individual actions in a free society. This is the only fair policy.

The Individual

An individual distinguishes himself in a free society through his or her attitude, diligence and effort. Yet, the effort by progressives to divide people into socially engineered collectives violates the principle of individual autonomy and creates conflict and other grievances.

As we discussed above, what matters is choice, volition, and extra effort on the individual scale. Anyone, of any skill, size and level of competence can exert high degrees of effort that defy physical strength, dexterity, stamina and other differences; but he must be free of collective chains and propaganda.

In other words, divisive social "trends" cannot inform social policy to any significant degree because they cause more harm compared to "so-called" utopian dreams. The individual will always "defy" these trends by choosing for him- or herself. For instance, there are no studies which measure the positive consequences of the exertion of volitional choice (it has simply never occurred to technocrats to study such a concept). All humans have volition, but so far, it has not received statistical analysis because progressives would rather study skin color and gender and other invented forms of discrimination.

Further, you can't expect all employees to think the same (liberal or conservative). Each individual decides how to think based upon the depth of his volitionally-attained knowledge, his upbringing and/or chosen values. For any individual, what makes one different from another is how much good knowledge he or she integrates into life and philosophy. Both genders and all "races" look at the same reality. Society can influence this for better or worse, but, ultimately, the individual decides for him- or herself and is responsible for his or her own thinking.

It is also not true that liberals/progressives represent the better philosophy when compared to conservatives. Conservatives and progressives merely represent two false sides of the same bankrupt coin of modern philosophy. One side is skepticism (progressivism) which holds the false view that man is incapable of understanding reality and the other (conservatism) holds the false view that knowledge is derived from a spiritual realm. Both views are wrong. Yet, each of them decides (without reason) that the other side is wrong which creates a vicious cycle of two sides both advocating the wrong ideas into perpetuity.

Yet, there are consequences to race- and gender-based divisions. They all miss the individual and therefore they discriminate in one way or another. Therefore, collectivism fails to bring about "social" goals. "Google's left-leaning tendencies make us blind to this bias and uncritical of its results, which they are using to justify their highly politicized programs"[1] This means that diversity policies will always be discriminatory in some way (such as discrimination against the competent).

Collectivism always misses its targets because it divides men into oppressors and victims. Today, an individual may be a victim while tomorrow, he may be an oppressor. There is no way to adequately identify these kinds of differences among individuals because of the destructive (progressive/liberal) practice of blaming sexism and racism where they do not exist. Their enemies are almost always competent people.

I disagree with Damore that diversity is a good thing. On the contrary, it is very bad and impossible to implement because there is no way to understand it; the idea must be constantly changing to accommodate changing political priorities. It fosters pragmatism which has no moral core and it does not even know that its claim to practical political action is a false notion.

The only way to eliminate sexism and racism in society is to stop interfering with merit-based hiring and promotion in corporations. Judging individuals according to merit is the best way for every individual to know the rules of the game; and they are simple: produce and prosper. And on *this* point, I agree with Damore: "treat people as

---

[1] Damore

individuals..." And, when it comes to "viewpoint diversity" the best policy is to let "the best ideas win and reward them". A merit-based system is also the best way to eliminate the "ideological echo chamber" and protect human accomplishment while eliminating political bias (like firing Damore).

Collectivism

Modern collectivism preaches a doctrine of capitalist racism. Under the influence of this view, anybody could claim racism and win huge victories against corporations in the universities and courtrooms. This is why some companies, over time, developed diversity programs. Assuming the veracity of the left's charges, they wanted to ensure that "capitalist flaws" did not lead to prejudice and discrimination against certain "groups".

For much of the 20th century, an atmosphere developed throughout society, the government, legal professions, universities and media that corporations must show racial consciousness and racial preferences lest they lose favor in the marketplace and government contracts. The implication of this social atmosphere was that, without scrutiny and law suits, corporations could get away with anything in the pursuit of profits.

I must ask the question, "Is capitalism, as an economic system, fraught with ethnic and racial discrimination?" In other words, is racism an integral feature of capitalism as Marxists claim? Is capitalism racist? Or is the racism that we sometimes see in society a residue, not of capitalism, but of the pre-capitalist eras?

Capitalism is Anti-racism

Before the advent of capitalism, society in Europe was decidedly class-oriented. The class system was monarchical which included a royal class, a lordly class which, along with the royal class, owned most of the power and then the lower classes who had very few rights.

"No free man shall be seized or imprisoned, or stripped of his rights or possessions, or outlawed or exiled . nor will we proceed with force against him . except by the lawful judgement of his equals or by the law of the land. To no one will we sell, to no one deny or delay right or justice."[2]

With these words, began a long period of intellectual development that led, eventually, to free market capitalism. That development culminated eventually to the concept of individual rights.

""The natural liberty of man consists in not recognizing any sovereign power on earth, and not be subject to the will or legislative authority to anyone."[3]

With these words, the Founding Fathers of the USA justified their building a nation upon the concept we know today as individual rights. The result of this philosophical development was the creation of a

---

[2] Magna Carta 1215 A.D.

[3] John Locke

limited government and the establishment of freedom or capitalism. Capitalism was further explained by Adam Smith in his book "The Wealth of Nation" which postulated that freedom resulted in a metaphorical "hidden hand". The principles of free market capitalism were born.

The distinctive characteristic of free market capitalism is that the class system was destroyed and any individual, regardless of station, could ascend the ladder of success. Anyone could become rich by careful management and investment of capital. Because man had individual rights, he could exert reason to the highest degree possible to himself and "make all the right moves", so to speak; he could raise capital, invest it and reap the benefits. It didn't matter what color he was, he could become rich through diligent work and effort.

There were, however, as with any great shift in ideas, those who did not fully understand the importance of the concept that capitalism had wiped out the class structure. Men still had volition and some of them still believed in a modified class system. These came into the capitalist system with their own pseudo-scientific views. One of these views was a new form of class structure which misinterpreted the views of Charles Darwin and postulated blood as a new class system. These views were common throughout much of the time when capitalism was eliminating all forms of classism. These "residues" of classism influenced the prevailing ideas in many European cultures for the worse.

I suggest that there is no feature endemic to capitalism that is racist. In fact, capitalism is one of the major factors, throughout history, that resulted in the elimination of racism because it liberated individuals to engage in rational economic acts. There is no tenet of capitalism that fosters, suggests or even rewards racist behavior. In fact, racist behavior is harmful to corporations and inimical to profit-seeking. In other words, because capitalism punishes irrational behavior in the market place, it also punishes companies engaged in racism.

I know that the idea of capitalism is very unpopular. Most progressives cannot fathom the idea that capitalism is anti-racist because they are influenced by their teaches who have told them that capitalism possessed endemic flaws such as racism and despotism. They falsely blamed capitalism for racism because the propagandists of anti-capitalism have fed them a lie. In fact, the left, was once an admirer of fascism which was the most racist system of the modern age. They saw fascism as a superior form of government and championed it here in America. They changed their view only because of the racist atrocities of Europe. Yet, they still foster the notions of centralized government.

But, I submit, they are wrong to assign racism to a capitalist system that is "endemically" anti-racist. One could say that capitalism was invented to be the only fair economic system in history. Here's why:

Capitalism *is* the "market system". This means that in all matters in which individuals transact money, make purchasing choices and plan their futures, unfair practices tend to work to the detriment of the individual or corporation that practices them. Capitalism rewards rational behavior; and treating people fairly, regardless of their skin color is rational behavior. In fact, treating people fairly improves production, improves earnings and improves market position for any individual or corporation that makes it a habit to do so.

What does it mean that (under capitalism) merit determines economic outcomes? It means that each individual is free to make his buying decisions based upon his self-interest; and through this process, he selects for purchase the highest quality in products and services. It is the buyer's merit that influences the merit of the producer of products and services. If he makes the right choice in his purchases, he will benefit more than those who make the wrong choice. If he is proficient at finding the best products and services, he influences the lives of those who produce them and makes them affluent.

Ayn Rand, an advocate of unfettered capitalism (which is the only form of capitalism) has pointed out that it was the industrial north that fought the civil war against the agrarian south. It was capitalism that needed labor and was willing to fight to liberate the slaves of the south. Once slavery was abolished, a mass migration of newly free people began moving into the industrial north.

The goal of the progressives (Republican and Democrat), after World War 2, was to regulate capitalism to skim profits and bring them into their own pockets. One of the arguments they used was that capitalism was responsible for racism. Using Marxist principles, they appropriated the term "liberal" and stole the anti-racist calls coming from true liberals (who were arguing for capitalism) and turned the liberal/progressive movement into one fostering centralized government. In principle and in practice, the new liberals (progressives) were advocates of the same centralized government fostered by the Nazis and communists while pretending to be anti-racist. The cat had changed his stripes.

The above facts of history have been totally obscured by the progressives who dominate our educational system. Any time you try to learn more about this period, through Google, you will find a plethora of articles that claim capitalism to be the cause of racism, the cause of poverty and the cause of an oppressive upper class. What you are reading is a wholesale attempt to keep you from learning the real nature and essence of capitalism which is the fact that capitalism is the most efficient and fair system ever invented on this planet. It is responsible for doubling life-expectancy and bringing unprecedented amounts of wealth and happiness to men who would have been "plebs" or commoners in other eras.

What you read in such articles are the so-called "flaws" of capitalism; that it has led to a separation of rich and poor, depletion of minerals, sexism, racism, and they have even compared capitalism to the plantation system, making laborers into slaves. The flaws of capitalism, in their view, make it necessary to control capitalism and regulate the actions of business people. The truth is that capitalism is not racist, does not deplete the planet and does not cause poverty. It is all the systems before capitalism that caused these factors and it is capitalism that is in the process of undoing the damage caused by the monsters of progressive philosophies (fascism, communism, welfare-statism). Capitalism is the answer to classism.

The progressives, trained in the universities, have learned the scam. They constantly find flaws in economic systems and declare that something needs to be done. Many of us have been brainwashed into the idea that these "politicians" are trying to help us against an oppressive capitalism. The truth is that they have found a way to get rich. By fostering laws that interfere in capitalist systems, they have founded a scam that lets them skim profits from corporations; political contributions, bribes and extortion. That is what our political system is all about. It is not about fighting capitalism; it is about money laundering.

Yet, today, we do not have a capitalist system. We have a mixed system because, as a society, we have been taught in our schools a mixed set of ideas. We have been told that too much capitalism is dangerous, and we need to coercively regulate it. This is why you see so much criticism of capitalism among progressives of the left and the right. This is why you find so many articles via Google from people who claim to find flaws in capitalism. The mixture of force and freedom in society is nothing more than a compromise between good and evil in the name of "the good". This compromise, this mixing of ideas, leads us to compromise with the very evil men who under cover of darkness are planning new ways to skim our money and keep it for themselves.

We allow this because we believe these lies about capitalism. We do not understand what capitalism is and we, as voters, put these monster into power.

Capitalism is essentially freedom. Because our government, supposedly, is charged with defending our individual rights, we gain the freedom to let our rational choices determine what we make and purchase. These everyday decisions make us affluent but only if we have a system that is not stealing millions from us daily. If we knew that the best thing for us is to get the politicians out of our pockets, to stop the looting of our money, we would clamor, not for more regulations but for one simple regulation: that politicians make no law that interferes with private activities. This would stop the looting. In other words, capitalism, being the solution to poverty, class and racism, should be fully capitalist, fully unfettered. Then we could make rational decisions and improve our lives without the children of Hitler stealing from us. Unfettered capitalism is the solution to mixed, compromised thinking.

For example, if I am a writer, I need the services of a good search engine to find the best knowledge available so I can produce a better book, article, play or poem, etc. If there is a search engine that consistently delivers this information to me, I will use that engine and no others. As a result, this search engine will be a better magnet for advertising and other services that can be offered to me and I benefit even more from using it. This search engine "merits" my business and it will prosper if it gives me what I need more consistently.

It does not matter the skin color of the maker of products or services I use. The only thing that matters is quality, productivity and effort. The same applies to corporations in their hiring practices. Merit determines the individuals hired by the company because merit creates the best outcomes for the corporation. If a corporation hires people based upon the color of their skin (or their gender), the likelihood is that it will hire people who do not provide the quality, productivity and effort that would make the company successful. This is because it must ignore merit and utilize a different standard that has nothing to do with competence.

Yet, if my search engine consistently delivers information whose goal is to socially-adjust me, to re-condition me to accept its egalitarian philosophy, it is not doing its job. It is making judgments on what they consider to be in my self-interest and it is, in effect, blocking the material I want – the truth. I don't mind if it presents all sides of an issue, but I do mind when it takes a stand and keeps me from seeing opposing views.

This has a spill-over in society. It is akin to the kind of censorship imposed upon mankind by the Catholic Church in its fight against science. By establishing the premise that "the secular" was the evil, it prohibited people from exploring nature and its characteristics. This effectively blocked people from thinking secularly and the result was the squalor of the medieval era. This tactic of blocking an opposing view is decidedly anti-science. Today, the idea of blocking knowledge from reaching people is un-American and defacto censorship.

When Marxist activists accuse corporations of being racist in their hiring standards, they are suggesting that corporations have "systemic" racism built into their natures as "for-profit" organizations. And they imply that racism is rational; they think that racist corporations benefit in the marketplace. Then they advocate that corporations "make up for their systemic racism" by establishing quotas that result in unfairness to workers of other races. This is a cognitive mistake on the part of "civil rights" advocates of the Marxist variety. It doesn't work that way in the real world.

Egalitarianism

To understand the scam that is being played on us, I decided to do a Goggle search on what is egalitarianism. Here is what I found in the first link (Investopedia):

"DEFINITION of 'Egalitarianism'

Egalitarianism is a philosophical thought system that emphasizes equality and equal treatment across gender, religion, economic status and political beliefs. Egalitarianism may focus on income inequality and distribution, which are ideas that influenced the development of various economic and political systems. Karl Marx looked to egalitarianism as a starting point in the creation of his Marxist philosophy, and John Locke considered egalitarianism when he proposed that individuals had natural rights.

"BREAKING DOWN 'Egalitarianism'

One of the major tenets of egalitarianism is all people are fundamentally equal. Egalitarianism can be examined from a social perspective that looks at ways to reduce economic inequalities, or from a political perspective that looks at ways to ensure the equal treatment and rights of diverse groups of people."

My first thought upon reading this is that there is a contradiction here. First, being politically equal is not the same as being equal in income. Yet, the author has conflated the two types of equality and called them both egalitarianism. There is a method to the madness.

The idea that men have equal rights refers to their equality in acting; that is, they are equal in how the law treats their actions. All men deserve justice – to be treated equally in the eyes of the law and the courts.

The idea of equality of result is entirely different. It means that some men have a claim to the property and/or values of other men. This is a violation of the principle of equality before the law. To take from one man to improve the result of another violates the individual rights of those citizens whose values are taken from them.

I argue for true egalitarianism which means that the government should have no power of expropriation, no right to take from law abiding citizens and give to others. Yet, today's egalitarians have no problem with expropriation. They consider it to be a form of justice.

When progressives demand that corporations pay people more money than they are worth (through minimum wages), they are suggesting that the corporations lose market position and competitive strength. The pass-through here can only start with the customer who must pay higher prices for products and services. The income from these higher prices are then transferred to government that decides who will receive these funds. That it is done by law is a travesty, unfair and harmful.

Likewise, when corporations must hire unqualified people because they should favor certain groups, egalitarians suggest that corporations lose market position and competitive strength. They are demanding that the corporation not only lose money but also that it pay money to less deserving employees. On the other hand, the individual who brings merit, in effect, is having his production re-distributed to those who do less and earn less for the corporation. *This* is unfairness.

The overall philosophy of those who accuse capitalism of being racist is egalitarianism, the idea that "social leveling" is more important than individual fairness and that "social justice" is more important than employee competence. This form of egalitarianism also holds that group identity (also called multi-culturalism) is more important than the individual and his or her identity. In effect, this view ignores the role of the individual as a factor in a corporation and it falsely replaces the individual with the group. This is a major reversal in the importance of individual competence to the success of corporations. It is a destructive concept that can only bring capitalism and affluence down.

For progressive egalitarians, human ability is non-existent; it isn't considered a factor in the success of a company. More than this, egalitarianism holds that you can ignore the actual causes of corporate success such as intelligence, individuality, excellence and performance. Their goal is to enact another cause, which is the melding of all individuals into a group. Further, because egalitarianism requires altruism (self-sacrifice), the prime value of the company, rather than being competence, becomes self-sacrifice.

This is what I call a "progressive" company; it is one characterized by the idea that to be successful the company must implement collectivism and altruism as fundamental principles. It must absorb the damage caused by incompetence and it must exploit competence to facilitate that absorption. When the profits start to diminish, they must look everywhere for enemies in order to avoid the simple fact that they have become an enemy of their customers. They will blame racism, sexism and other forms of bigotry in order to avoid responsibility.

Consider that collectivism and altruism do not bring about production and profits. In fact, they discourage people from being productive while they exhort the most competent workers to sacrifice for the less competent. They ask the productive individual to work harder in order to make up for the losses suffered at the hand of the incompetent who are considered to have some sort of grievance.

In a progressive company, collective standards prevail. Rather than ignoring skin color, the managers of the progressive organization *consider* skin color and develop quotas to "represent" the so-called racial makeup of the community. Rather than hire the best workers regardless of color, the progressive company will hire workers *because* of skin color to give the impression of being a forward-looking company that treats people fairly.

But is hiring according to skin color fair? What about the worthy other-heritage individual who was not hired because hiring him or her would cause an imbalance in the color quotas? This individual could be highly competent, perhaps more competent than all other individuals, perhaps even a future CEO of the company who discovers something revolutionary. Where is the fairness in not hiring this individual? The company is robbing itself of the substantial benefit of his or her employ.

Consider also the impact of the employee without education and ability who is hired because he falls into the color quota. Because he has little in the way of innate ability, the company must suffer productive losses in order to give the appearance of fairness. He is getting the job that would have gone to the worker who is more competent several times over. How does this benefit the company? How does it benefit the unqualified individual who will fail in some important way? I have seen these individuals fired after months or even years of trying to "make" them fit in. Once he or she is gone, the company must hire another similar person and go through the process of loss all over again.

By hiring the best employees regardless of ethnicity or gender, the company would benefit more while companies that hired according to gender and ethnicity would be unable to serve the customer effectively.

Long before the age of racial quotas, the race and gender egalitarians made the argument that the "best" employees of color or gender were being excluded because of "systemic" bias that was embedded in the culture. The truth was that, by this time, most companies were already hiring qualified minorities because they wanted the *best* employees they could find in the marketplace. It was progressive egalitarianism that interfered in that process and forced companies to lose customers.

While the egalitarians were calling for quotas, many corporations were already "color-blind" in their hiring practices. Despite this, the egalitarians advocated forcing corporations to hire according to racial, ethnic and gender standards. This required that the company ignore college performance, aptitudes and other measures based upon merit because these measures supposedly had a built-in cultural bias.

But egalitarians were so certain of the evil of capitalism that anything done to thwart profit-

making companies was deemed worthy. Forcing
capitalist entities to violate their own self-interests
was thought to be a viable way to advance "people
over profits". They wrongly thought that this
approach would inflict no appreciable damage to
corporations.

How to Destroy a Company

There is only one way to ensure that a company stays successful and that is to hire and reward the best thinkers and hardest workers regardless of skin color. Equalizing employees in ways that disregard individual achievement is the best way to ensure that the best employees leave the company. In fact, the only employees that would stay at such a company are those who contribute less and want to benefit from the poor hiring practices. They would be employees who advocate the sacrifice of the best to the least and who *are* the least. They are essentially free riders waiting for the eventual demise of the company.

The demise of the company begins immediately upon the announcement that the company intends to hire according to a principle other than merit. This is because the intelligent employee knows that his contribution is singular and deserving. If you don't pay him or her based upon the value created; if you don't want him or her to contribute *productively*, then you will lose him or her and your competitor will gain.

Egalitarians constantly ignore the efficacy, and especially the importance, of intelligence and hard work. They think that all they need to do is preach altruism and convince productive employees that they should, as a matter of morality, contribute their hard work to the groups that the company has placed upon a collective pedestal. The truth is that altruistic arguments, forcibly imposed, no matter how wistfully preached, only mean one thing; that the productive employee will not be able to improve his own life through his own hard work. This is the best way to destroy loyalty and eliminate competence. It is the start of a downward cycle.

Taking it to the Street

The company that inserts egalitarian principles into its mission must necessarily become wedded to egalitarian solutions in society. If you believe your company's moral fabric should include egalitarian principles, then you have no choice but to want those ideas to spread throughout society. Ideas that oppose progressive egalitarianism, no matter how reasonable, must not be allowed to see the light of day.

For instance, in Google's case, the company will think its responsibility to society is to feed links that foster egalitarianism. It will do this as a matter of clear thinking, of logic, and even scientific veracity, to such a degree that it will foster only links that validate egalitarianism in society. It may throw a bone to some other opposing ideas, but it will not give these ideas any degree of prominence. Or it will make sure that such materials include scholarly doubt and that peer-reviewed works reject them. They will find materials that mention only a few opposition arguments and isolate the good points as part of a larger discredited concept. There will never be an "integrated" presentation of the opposing views, only discretely applied slices of it, much like an apple whose pieces are separated from the core.

They do not even think it possible that egalitarianism is wrong. Employees are obliged to believe, as a matter of principle, that only leftist / progressive / egalitarian policies bring value to the customers. But there is a difference between productive value offered to customers and social engineering. One brings income, the other brings frustration to customers.

The real question is "what if egalitarianism is evil?" What kind of company does that make the organization? At the very least it will be a company willing to let its own cognitive inefficacy become policy. It will be wedded to the unfairness of egalitarianism in the name of fairness. It will be an enemy of people yearning to be free. Yet, the government will eagerly hold Google's feet to the fire and make it practice what it preaches.

Egalitarianism is evil. It presents a major contradiction to society, not the least of which is that egalitarians believe that the end justifies the means. The end, a so-called "fair" society, requires re-distribution from earners to those who have not earned their own keep. Employees think that any deceptive means is justified so long as the end is considered good. But this puts them in a position where they must eventually believe that force exerted against individuals is the only way to achieve a good end.

Aristotle declares that there are certain "natural" ends toward which the motions of entities move. This teleological approach applies to the nature of reality and how it works. The ends fostered by egalitarians, on the other hand, are chosen "man-made" ends, and this requires that those ends be "practical" which means produce the ends desired. In the case of egalitarian ends, that standard has not been met.

Egalitarians hold their "ends", various forms of equality, as floating abstractions with no connection to efficient causes. Therefore, egalitarianism never accomplishes its end; and, most importantly, this is why their only recourse is to force egalitarianism upon otherwise free individuals. The idea of "from each according to his ability, to each according to his needs" becomes an impossible principle. To foster the destruction of the ends of some people (the able) for the sake of others (the needy) results in the destruction of both the able and the needy. History has proven this and there is virtually no example of a sustainable altruistic transaction. The egalitarian answer? "In the long-run, we're all dead."

The End Justifies the Means

Egalitarianism is essentially a platonic construct that has nothing to do with attainable ends. It posits an "out there" end (from Plato's realm of essences) without any achievable "worldly" means. In such a situation, there is no way to bring the end about; so, lacking a practical and benign means, the only way of accomplishing the end, according to the technocrats of egalitarianism, is to use force or coercion against individuals; to essentially make slaves out of them, to order expropriation of their product for the sake of people who produce no product. This creates a "slave vs. beneficiary" social condition. The slave is unfairly converted to the status of an oppressor and punished while the beneficiary is herded into a protected collective that is worthy, because of invented grievances, to be gifted with the product of the slave.

Certainly, the egalitarians soothe themselves by proclaiming to be pragmatic doers who believe in practical results and who possess a genuine love for the "downtrodden". Their pragmatism (force) is couched in terms such as practical, results-oriented, concerned with only the possible, etc., etc., etc., all of which is untrue. In fact, the means they use, coercion, makes their goals impractical purely on the face of it. That they don't realize this gives the lie to their claims of being practical and scientific. The truth is, they have no idea what they are doing.

To justify expropriation, often called re-distribution, the government must provide a justification for its oppressive behavior toward the slave. The propaganda will inevitably be an altruistic plea for self-sacrifice on the part of the slave. Whether he agrees with the calls for altruism is irrelevant; it is the "right" thing to do, part of the social contract they think. So much for scientific technocracy.

In fact, the belabored "producer" of the benefit very seldom likes the idea of having his work taken from him without payment. Expropriation, even if it is called a "loving gift" requires force; and force is a negative; an act of violence.

And, the so-called practicality of technocracy is a delusion. The act of force has a negative impact upon the quality and quantity of the gift given. That is a scientifically provable fact that is seldom mentioned by the technocrats. This means that most often the benefit given to the aggrieved party does not actually achieve the desired result over a long period of time. The aggrieved beneficiary gains only the incentive to demand more benefits.

But, the whole process, because it is essentially based upon a materialistic construct (pie in the sky) that comes straight out of Hegelian/Marxist determinism, has no relation to the real world. It is essentially a blind projection of benefits that, in fact, do not come about. For the reasons mentioned above, the result of all egalitarian schemes is a breakdown of the altruistic transaction and impoverishment of the parties.

Apparently, the egalitarians at Google do not know this. They do not know that their efforts to "equalize" all employees and people in society will fail and result in many unhappy once-productive employees and an even larger number of entitled unproductive employees.

Division and Race in Society

Egalitarianism can only cause division in society. Google would call it progressive versus conservative (which division is a cognitive dead end). Certainly, the user/customer is not served by this division and the bias it creates and neither is society.

But this division goes beyond corporations who are afraid to anger government and so-called civil rights advocates. Those who want to "equalize" society will never see progress or fairness. They think they must constantly agitate grievances and constantly criticize and attack. Today, according to the race baiters, every white person is a racist, a member of the KKK and a hater.

Yet, racism is racism; it is a thought process, and anyone can commit it (regardless of color). The practice of assigning negative characteristics to one group of people based on skin color without consideration of individual qualities and opinions is racism. The color makes no difference. You cannot rightfully say that you are justified in being racist if you have experienced racism. What you should say, to yourself, is "how can I become a better employee who produces value for my company. That is the civil rights challenge of the 21st century. The days of protest and agitation are over.

Today, the USA is the least racist society in the history of the world, but the agitators for division are inventing new charges daily about racism. The point of creating race divisions is not to solve problems; but to cause problems that will frighten corporate executives into contributing millions of dollars for special "projects" intended to help minorities. Essentially, it is shakedown ala Alinsky.

Is there racism in society? As a Hispanic, I can truthfully say that I have seen it and experienced it. But the overall attitude in the business world is fairness and good will. As a manager, I managed both white and black supervisors and had working relationships with people of all colors. I knew it existed, I saw it, but it was not total; it was not everywhere and to say that racism is a big problem today is a lie. It is a problem but there are many good people of all colors who are eager to be fair and to give jobs to productive people of all colors.

If you are an individual in America today, your responsibility is to educate yourself, to become smart, to work hard, and to do your best. If you do those things, like many individuals have done, you can succeed. Complaining about race and being a constant agitator ignores the fact that the purpose of business is to do business; it is not to solve social problems or equalize society.

I have written elsewhere that racism is an individual problem, not a collective problem. Group thinking is collectivism and collectivism is the opposite of individualism. It is individuals who must learn what racism is and it is individuals whose minds must be changed. That is done through education, not through reparations and guilt-inducing behavior.

Certainly, there are many honest and rational civil rights advocates in society. They seek to educate young people on how to develop skills and negotiate for advancement in society. They base their opinions and actions on the concept of equality under the law and they seek to teach people how to demand their rights in a society where merit rules.

Others, are out and out extortionists who use race to shakedown corporations and enrich themselves by making outlandish claims against American corporations. These people do not help eliminate racism. In fact, the more power they gain, the more neighborhoods they ruin. When they come into a town, businesses move out. And then they call those businesses racist.

The atmosphere of fear in American corporations causes many of them to do exactly the wrong thing which is to capitulate and give into the demands of the race baiters. These Alinsky Radicals aren't out to help anyone; they are out for power and it is not about the neighborhoods or people, it is about them; their glorification and their power. The right thing to do is to resist this oppression and insist that the company hire by merit and merit alone.

Equal Pay

Imagine a situation in which the board members of Google decide that the proper end of society is income equality regardless of ability or productive output. This hypothetical leadership group is convinced that income equality is a "no brainer". Everyone should understand the logic of this and support income equality at Google.

What will happen is that every employee at the company will begin calculating the productive value he or she brings to the company and compare that value to the value of other employees. If the employee determines that he or she is producing far more value for the company than a large percentage of other employees, he or she may decide that the new policy is harmful and resign from the company.

If the employee calculates that his or her value is far less than most other employees, he or she may see that this scheme is unfair to those employees who produce more than most.

Yet, some employees will realize that they will be paid far more than they are worth and see the new policy as a boon and be very happy about getting an unearned paycheck. This employee will hang around until the company starts cutting dead weight.

Ask yourself how long will a company last when its best employees quit and/or decide to lower their production? Also ask yourself how long will the company last when the only employees who stay either don't want to be there or have no problem being paid more than they are worth? If you answer these questions correctly, you now know why egalitarianism does not work.

Customer Service

Continuing with this hypothetical, because they are not convinced that Egalitarianism divides employees, Google must, of necessity, conclude that all search results on the issue of income inequality should only be fed web pages that advocate Google's position on the issue. Any search results that foster the opposite view on merit-based hiring will be presented after those that advocate income re-distribution.

This last move is inevitable. The market position that Google earned at its start which fed the most relevant search results has now become subject to Google's market dominance for the supposed good of all.

Since our society is made up of people with various views on important issues, those who do not like Google's result policies will go elsewhere. Google must think, "Good riddance". Indeed, there are some people who do not appreciate Google deciding for them about desired search results. That Google considers itself the judge of correct thinking about conservative ideas is condescending to say the least. The anti-capitalist bias is palpable. Just "shut up" says Google.

On virtually every issue of contention today between progressives and conservatives, Google fills the browser with articles that argue against the conservative view. Many articles they offer are clearly Marxist and most assume that the progressives have the superior and more knowledgeable perspective on the issue. Google has joined the leftist media in providing us with "their truth".

I am not a conservative and I consider conservatives wrong on many issues because they often advocate altruism rather than individual rights. They "me-too" the progressives. The Google policy appears to be that only progressives have the right approach to most issues. There is no acknowledgment of the fact that there are a variety of views and that some well-argued dissenting views are worth being considered.

Force in Society

Force in society creates various forms of moral paralysis.

The first form of moral paralysis proceeds from the fear of being personally harmed by a robber or extortionist. When one knows that force is being used as a threat, one experiences fear, and this sometimes causes one to act contrary to how he (through reason) would otherwise prefer.

In a corporation, the damage from physical threats (from rioters at the executive's home and looming lawsuits (another form of extortion)) could be immense and cause serious financial losses to the company as well as psychological damage to employees who are forced to do things they consider unreasonable.

Secondly, there is government-induced paralysis caused by government controls and regulations. If individuals within a given company are told to act in a certain way because the government demands it, then there is no need for management to persuade employees about their behavior because a metaphorical gun controls the discussion.

One can see this process at play in companies such as Google when they feel compelled to hire a VP of Diversity to spout the "company" and government line about diversity being a top value of the company. In virtually every case of this type, companies create propaganda that is designed to depict forced diversity policies as something so wonderful (and scientific) that no "good" employee would disagree.

If you think that merit should rule in companies such as this, and you have good examples of how forced diversity is harming the workplace, then you are called "anti-social" and undeserving of a job. You don't fit in, despite the possibility that you might be right.

Government force supersedes human autonomy by removing it as a factor in business decision making. Additionally, the government ignores the fact that business owners and employees are autonomous individuals; they should be free to make the business decisions that reason dictates. No individual (and no corporation) can thrive without freedom of thought and action.

With force as a factor in society, the principle of inverse variation[4] tells us that as force increases, the amount of thinking that the individual does decreases. This is the paralysis which I mentioned before. If actions are forced in one specific area, the individual is paralyzed in that area. As the force increases (along a continuum from minimal force to total force), then the amount of rational thinking possible eventually decreases to zero. This creates

---

[4] "For two quantities with inverse variation, as one quantity increases, the other quantity   decreases."
Source https://www.varsitytutors.com/hotmath/hotmath_help/topics/inverse-variation

lackluster performance, reduces innovation and destroys competitive strength. This principle applies to individuals, corporations, governments and entire societies.

Yet, it is also true that the longer a given level of force is exerted upon an individual or corporation, the debilitating impact of that force grows exponentially due to the absence of freedom. This is because people are not allowed to collaborate, investigate and grow their knowledge over time which results in less innovation and less quality over time.

We see this process in totalitarian societies where the government progressively monitors and controls all private thoughts and decisions in the name of social justice. This is the zero-end of the impact of force in society and it is the direction in which our society is descending because of egalitarianism.

In a situation in which government progressively exerts force, the society tends to be corrupted over time. Eventually, we arrive at a situation like that seen in the novel 1984 by George Orwell. Here, truth becomes the pronouncements of government and has less and less to do with reality and more to do with the "need" of government to control the thoughts and actions of individuals. Words change meanings constantly, eventually referring to their opposites.

The lives of individuals become empty and meaningless while the existence of the state becomes the highest value celebrated by fake enthusiasm and a false need to conciliate the government and worship its leaders.

Google has put itself into the position of fostering a propagandized egalitarianism that is based upon force (fascism and/or socialism) and it imposes upon employees and society a view that considers individual rights to be meaningless. In such a propagandized system, the people are not supposed to believe the truth they experience; they are supposed to believe that everything is great. They learn to accept decline and decay as examples of stability and they think that, despite their own lives, the "lives of others" must be constantly getting better. Eventually, the truth of decline is so overwhelming that the individual must not only lie to himself, but also to everyone he knows. When a "man on the street" reporter asks him for his opinion, he spouts the government lies and pretends to be happy.

It is this condition that begins inside a company as soon as it takes on a VP of Diversity. Everyone in the company must agree with the "pie in the sky" pronouncements and declare themselves the beneficiaries of these "wonderful" policies. If you don't agree with the logic of diversity policies, then, the company executives (and government) must think, society should re-condition and re-educate you.

The fact is, people don't like to be forced and companies that force-feed ideas to employees lead eventually to government-approved ideas. This cannot end well for a company that once offered real value to its customers - by giving them what they wanted.

If you think that giving in to government policies on the issue of diversity is a small thing of little consequence, consider the full range of egalitarian demands. As Dr. Peikoff says,

"In place of the traditional idea of justice as giving every man his due which implies that some are due more than others, we must implement a new definition of justice—justice as fairness. Fairness here means the elimination of the results of Nature's unfairness.

"Besides inequality of wealth, there are many other sorts of inequality that egalitarians in various areas condemn as unfair and seek to remove. Today's ethnic leaders, who regard opponents of the new fairness as racist, seek not old-fashioned civil rights, already long gained, but equality for their minorities in regard to all the values enjoyed by the majority. Feminists seek equality with males—in income, status, power—through liberation from "sexism." Age activists, fighting "ageism," want equality with the young. The physically handicapped, fighting "ableism," want equality with the healthy. The ugly, fighting "looksism," want equality with the beautiful. The multiculturalists, fighting "imperialism," want the West to acknowledge that its culture is no better than any other. The animal-rights activists, fighting "speciesism," want us to recognize that man is no more important than any other creature."[5] Add to this the demands of environmentalists for a "green" company and you have a nightmare of unreasonable demands and constantly switching irrational claims.

How can any corporation's management possibly deal with all these "isms" except by rejecting them and insisting that they run their businesses according to reason? How can they let their businesses be hijacked and diverted from their mission if they must consider the demands of these groups in their hiring and decision making? The truth is that for today's manager, the critical factor in success is service to the customer and not special-interests who want to muscle-in on their profits.

Progressives believe that if you are a pro-capitalist who advocates the Bill of Rights and the Constitution, there is something wrong with you. At the very least they think you are unscientific and logically corrupt. At the worst, you are racist and evil. They claim to be champions of the right ideas and believe they can bring about prosperity through scientific technocracy. They proclaim the practical nature of their ideas but blame capitalism whenever their ideas fail; and they always fail. From Nazi Germany, to Communist China, their adherence to force in society brings about the destruction in mass

---

[5] The DIM Hypothesis by Leonard Peikoff, Egalitarianism, Page 173

numbers of the productive contingent in society. Yet, they claim that this destruction is not their fault. They have the right ideas but the wrong leaders they tell us after every social failure.

There is a fundamental reason for their failures and it is not capitalism; it is coercion, force. Their regulation of society, their technocratic control is what causes failure, not capitalism's freedom.

And Google has become one of history's largest proponents of regulatory schemes. Their false advocacy of coercion in society is a key cause of society's failure and will also be the cause of Google's decline. For instance, progressives at Google think that "pro-capitalist" categories do not deserve to be placed at the top of any search result. I suggest that you perform a Google search on the term "egalitarianism versus capitalism" and you'll get a list of links, virtually all of which foster egalitarianism while distorting the meaning and social consequences of capitalism.

One fact that none of these articles will mention is that egalitarianism requires force against individuals. Even the Investopedia definition that we found before does not mention this aspect of egalitarianism when it declares:

"Egalitarianism is a philosophical thought system that emphasizes equality and equal treatment across gender, religion, economic status and political beliefs. Egalitarianism may focus on income inequality and distribution, which are ideas that influenced the development of various economic and political systems. Karl Marx looked to egalitarianism as a starting point in the creation of his Marxist philosophy, and John Locke considered egalitarianism when he proposed that individuals had natural rights."[6]

As we can see with this definition, the form of egalitarianism fostered by progressives is ambiguous. Marxism and its derivatives held that people had equal rights, but they also fostered a "solution" that government should advance "social justice" by means of violating rights. This meant that some people were robbed of their rights for the sake of others. This led to a collectivist social framework in which some people were treated as equal members of a group while others were required to work on their behalf. The leaders of such collectives were authority figures who could "direct", that is, force, a fair distribution of results by insisting that productive members perform to a higher standard than non-productive members. This is not equality.

Another form of egalitarianism fostered by individual rights advocates holds that all men are equal in terms of their treatment by the legal system. It fosters individual rights which means that no one (government or the individual) could encroach on the

---

[6] https://www.investopedia.com/terms/e/egalitarianism.asp#ixzz52bTIGU2k

rights of all men. It denies the existence of any collective obligation on the part of individual. It disallows government force of any type except force which defends the individual in the pursuit of happiness. Egalitarians claim that this is oppressive but note that no force is involved in the liberation of the individual. And, contrary to the claims of egalitarians, this form of society does not create poverty but instead lifts "all boats", so to speak. Even the lives of poor people are made better by capitalism.

Marxist and progressive egalitarianism require the suppression of natural or acquired qualities in a person in order to re-distribute the benefits of those qualities to people who do not possess them. This not only applies to income but even to virtue. Egalitarianism steals virtue and re-distributes its results to the non-virtuous. It represents a fundamental attack on individuals under the premise that any individual with abilities or good fortune does not deserve them. It is a false notion that results in exploitation, moral extortion and corruption. And this is why socialism and communism fail.

The Marxist/progressive form of egalitarianism declares that good personal qualities are properties of the group and not of the individual. It declares that the group has a right to re-distribute, through force, those qualities to those who do not possess them.

There are two types of force in society. First there is physical force which is put forward by authorities and criminals who say, "if you don't do what I say, you'll be punished or killed", and then there is moral force which is put forward by people who say, "if you don't sacrifice for others, you'll be labeled as evil and punished (in Hell or on earth). Both forms of force leave the individual depressed and persecuted. For the (productive) individual, under the weight of both types of force, motivation dies and there is no reason to try to prosper in such a society.

Certainly, the level of force in society is an indicator that will help us weigh the presence or lack of initiative in society. Generally, the more extreme the force exerted by government and criminal elements, the more extreme the lack of initiative. In fact, the more force you introduce into an organization or society, the less initiative you have.

In any egalitarian corporation or society, employees eventually tire of mouthing enthusiastic support for "levelling the playing field". They tire of tribal divisions and protests that support those divisions.

By advancing largely artificial divisions such as skin color, ethnicity and other forms of collectivism, the company (or society) becomes "politicized"; a prey of the politician seeking a shakedown or a contribution. As we saw above, a conflict arises between the individuals who are openly exploited and the self-entitled individuals seeking the undeserved. Eventually, the company (or the society) will be managed according to the dictates of government.

This is where Google stands today, and this is why you see such oppressive behavior toward individuals like James Damore and his silenced former associates. Management must be enthusiastic in fostering its diversity policies because they know that the government can come down upon them at any moment for virtually anything they do. They are afraid.

In fact, it does little good to engage in detailed studies about the impact of gender or race bias in society. It does little good to fear the "advance" of certain groups at the expense of "my group". This is because the operative bias is neither race nor gender; on the contrary, the operative bias is force as it is imposed upon corporations (the business / government alliance) and on individuals who work for those corporations.

A corporation in a presumably free economy requires the ultimate in economic liberty. Force and liberty are opposites and when liberty is denied, individuals cannot take the actions their reasoning minds would otherwise take. This creates bad decisions, losses and dissatisfaction (paralysis) among corporate management, employees and, eventually, customers – all while corporate leaders travel the country telling us about the brave new world that collectivism and egalitarianism will bring. Do they know that they are lying? Do they know that this brave new world will never come about? All they know is that if they use their power to skew the search parameters in the favor of socialism and egalitarianism, the government will not take them over. Or so they think. Like the capitalists who sell the communists the rope that will be used to hang them, companies like Facebook and Google think that if they are "good little boys" the Master will allow them to play in the sandbox. This is the lie they tell themselves.

Adjusting gender and race hiring is not only impractical, it is downright destructive of the corporation's long-term market position. This is because those adjustments destroy the ability of individuals to prosper according to their merits. In fact, technocratic studies that preach race and gender preferences are fruitless. They are pseudo-science fraught with racism and gender bias whose real victims are individuals. A society capable of seeing through the racists of the past is today incapable of seeing its own biases.

The existence of a particular bias (let's say color-bias in this case) cannot be accurately measured simply because many decisions in corporations are still based upon logic and merit rather than skin color. Therefore, any "color-driven" decisions imposed by egalitarians create a confirmation bias that is racist. When every decision is lumped into one thought process, namely that every disparity is an example of race or gender bias, we wind up with faulty data and the inability to forecast cause and effect. We are also left, eventually, with one culprit, and today, for progressives, that culprit is white males and "their" capitalist system. Yet, through some twist of logic, this is thought to be a scientifically proven notion. It is not. It is good old-fashioned racism.

Indeed, the technocrats in corporations and government are characterized by their biases against individuals (the individual doesn't matter to them) and capitalism (capitalism is evil or ineffective or racist). Don't try to question their data; you'll get fired. "These practices are based upon false assumptions generated by our biases and can actually increase race and gender tensions. We're told by senior leadership that what we're doing is both the morally and economically correct thing to do, but without evidence this is just veiled left ideology that can irreparably harm Google." (Damore)

The Fallacy of Egalitarianism

Why are diversity policies wrong for corporate America? They are essentially unfair to people with abilities and initiative. The idea that talented people owe something to untalented is simply wrong. Nature is not fair and there is no reason why the results of hard work and initiative should be sacrificed by those who bring them about. The effort to equalize results is an unfair idea that only a collectivist would concoct.

The false premise of egalitarianism is that collectivism trumps individualism and this discrimination brings unfairness into the actions of American corporations. This is because egalitarianism defines the individual out of existence. It glorifies the "group" as if the term were a magical entity that will achieve some sort of wonderful goal. When the goal does not materialize, people can only insist that the government exert more controls until it is virtually running the corporation.

Eventually, the government will nationalize the tech industry in the name of the public good (And the biggest lie will be that capitalism has failed again). In fact, what will have failed are the very government controls that egalitarians insisted upon. With every failure of government regulation, people are locked into demanding more government regulation - a vicious downward cycle of economic despair takes place. You cannot achieve "the moral" by introducing re-distribution of any type. You must get the government out of corporate life and re-introduce merit-based policies if you want to save the company and society.

What happens when the government dictates hiring practices to a corporation? The entire culture of the corporation becomes an experimental program with constantly changing rules and standards. That's why large corporations need a VP of Diversity. Every day, they discover that their diversity policies create problems, so they must constantly be monitoring the negative impacts of diversity rules - you could call it "Diversity Whack-a-Mole".

Government officials think they can shakedown the company because it is "too big to fail". This is because they don't know anything about running a company. They only know how to shakedown profit-seeking executives. They roll out their litany of Marxist criticisms and false economic theories anytime they need a campaign contribution. Any political pronouncement the politician makes is a threat - here come the auditors and regulators.

What is lost in this egalitarian madness is a consideration of what is good for the corporation (and eventually for the employees). Corruption grows when nervous executives must be careful about everything they do in front of the prying eyes of government; the one thing they cannot do is criticize the government.

Corporate Fear

Diversity should not be a goal in any corporation. It should be the consequence of rational thinking on the part of management. In a free society, corporate managers are free to discuss their company's problems and come up with the best solutions. They look at the facts and speak their minds giving no thought to the censor.

On the other hand, if they live in a coercive society (communist, socialist, fascist), government force constantly looms as a threat. The censor/regulator judges them, directs them and punishes them whenever they disagree with government edicts.

Corporate managers are limited in what they can do because government has already decided what they and their employees must think; and if the managers disagree with the government about what is right for the company, their opinions do not matter. The government and its force rules. Corporate fear rules the company; not freely chosen opinions and policies.

Today, and for many decades now, the last thing executives (of virtually any major company) have wanted to admit is that they are looking out for the company. Instead they write articles and books that spout the government line about "giving back" to society and how much they care for the under-privileged. Through all this gibberish, they seek to ensure the public that they are dedicated to the government's goals. They praise politicians and ignore the slaves (American workers) that egalitarianism has created. They spout platitudes about "social justice" and declare their fervent desire to accomplish "fairness", not "dirty" profits.

Collectivism, in the form of egalitarianism, must inevitably find a scapegoat to destroy. For Google, that scapegoat is James Damore and any "conservative" who disagrees with the egalitarianism of the left. Armed with the idea that conservatives are racists, they feel justified in persecuting them. After all, they think, they are right when they say that conservatives are racists.

The legal filings presented by Damore indicate that Google is, in a sense, out of control. The leftist ideas of the extreme far left have liberated them to engage in some dastardly behavior. As the filings indicate, these behaviors include:

- Furnishing "internal mailing lists catering to employees with alternative lifestyles, including furries, polygamy, transgenderism, and plurality, for the purpose of discussing sexual topics. The only lifestyle that seems to not be openly discussed on Google's internal forums is traditional heterosexual monogamy."
- "(P)roposing hiring practices that exclude certain groups of men, or putting women in charge of hiring for a year to ensure diversity quotas are met. One employee wrote: "Alternate proposal: moratorium on hiring white cis heterosexual abled men who aren't abuse survivors.""

- "Damore recounts attending "voluntary" diversity training because Google employees stressed attendance as necessary if he were to advance in the company. "At the in-person training, entitled 'Bias Busting,' Google discussed how biases against women exist in the workplace, and how 'white male privilege' exists in the workplace," the suit reads. "The training was run by the 'Unbiasing Group' at Google."
- "After a coworker leaked his memo to the public, Google's human resources instructed Damore to work remotely for a while to let emotions cool, after he forwarded them a particularly angry email from another employee. "You're a misogynist and a terrible person," read a late-night email from Alex Hidalgo, a Google engineer. "I will keep hounding you until one of us is fired. Fuck you.""
- "The suit claims Gudeman was fired in part because he took issue with the merits of a "derail document" written by Google manager Kim Burchett. "The thesis of this document is that on this one particular set of topics, the left-wing political frame of systematic bias, must always dominate, and the receiver must accept that frame, and its associated worldview, in their response," the suit claims. It does not provide the actual document.
"In his response, Gudeman (Damore's co-complainant) said "the point of this document is to disallow any defense at all that a man might make when some woman complains about bias. There is no defense. The woman is always right. The man has no alternative but to submit to her superior

moral position. We have a word for that attitude, it's called 'sexism.'""

- "The suit includes a screenshot of one of the emailed "peer bonuses" awarded to those who opposed Damore."

- "'Discourage them all throughout the industry'
"If we really care about diversity in tech, we don't just need to chase serial offenders out of Google, we need to discourage them all throughout the industry," a lengthy internal post on Damore read. "We should be willing to give a wink and a nod to other Silicon Valley employers over terminable offenses, not send the worst parts of tech packing with a smile ..."""

- "Damore's memo prompted another employee to post this quote: "I'm a queer-ass nonbinary trans person that is fucking sick and tired of being told to open a dialogue with people who want me dead. We are at a point where the dialogue we need to be having with these people is 'if you keep talking about this shit, I will hurt you.'""

- "Google encourages employees to enforce unwritten norms by harassing and ostracizing those who break them, according to the suit, and by allowing employees to create "blocklists" on their communications systems. "[Google] relies on crowdsourced harassment and 'pecking' to enforce social norms (including politics) that it feels it cannot write directly into its policies," the suit states."[7]

Damore did not help himself when he claimed that women were emotionally different from men which is not provable scientifically. However, such a claim, though unprovable, is not sexist. It is merely miss-guided. I suspect that this issue will be raised in the upcoming trial.

As these charges indicate, the extreme forms of collectivism do not unite people but divide them into warring camps through which people of divergent principles are isolated, ostracized and "kicked out" of the corporation. Collectivism is a fantasy based on a myth. The fantasy is that collectivism leads to good things. The myth is that collectivism is a unifying principle.

The destruction of liberty and freedom of speech (especially) leads to total collapse of the corporate system. This is an instance of the law of cause and effect. If you divert a company from its basic mission through policies like diversity, you necessarily destroy the company because it cannot earn a profit. You staff the company with employees who are not dedicated to the corporate mission and you force them to pursue social goals that are antithetical to the

---

[7] Quotes provided in an article which appeared on The Federalist website (http://thefederalist.com/2018/01/10/19-insane-tidbits-james-damores-lawsuit-googles-office-environment/) written by Rachel Stoltzfoos. Internal quotes are from the lawsuit.

goals of the company. The new "collectivist" nature of the corporation causes capital to flee, services to decline and diversity of thought to die.

I have seen this process in a large corporation. It was thought that it could have productive employees by training them to foster diversity alone. Instead of merit hiring, they chose racial, ethnic and gender standards and tried to train those individuals to be service oriented. Training costs increased while service declined.

The workforce became diverse, but profits did not increase. Instead, large amounts of corporate capital were invested in dealing with grievances, low production and lost value. It became the job of the managers to make sure the employees where happy rather than productive. This situation so discouraged the managers that many of them left the company in frustration – including myself. My experience is anecdotal, but I think many corporate managers have experienced similar frustrations.

The emergence of diversity, collectivism and anti-capitalism in America's corporations represents poisons injected into the system. The last thing you get when a company abandon's reason in hiring and management is reason and good management. Like a living host, when you inject a deadly poison, the body dies. American corporations should only be about increasing value and that can only be done by production, good services and dedicated employees.

Entitlement, race and gender diversity and other such collectivist notions do not belong in a "for-profit" organization. Once they take hold, the corporation is ripe for a competitive challenge.

Yet, beyond the philosophical poison, the major culprit here is the government/business alliance. Because every business in such a system operates as an extension of the government, it is not possible for employees to focus on satisfying the customer. The diversity programs mentioned above represent a coercive demand that the company operate according to collective principles which include altruism, re-distribution and collective (class warfare) struggles for dominance and entitlement. These are imposed through government oversight, regulations, anti-trust lawsuits, audits and compliance reporting.

This alliance tells all institutions under the government's umbrella that "If you want the benefits of dealing with government, you will function according to government's rules". The institutions then open their doors, not only to government, but also to the technocrats and bureaucrats who intend to direct the class struggle within the corporation. The result is thought control and exclusion of anyone who refuses to do the goose-stepping march.

This process, extended throughout the largest corporations in the world, creates an economically dysfunctional world. Those who keep quiet about the imposition of force in society can survive and participate. Those who disagree are thrown out of the group and backed into a corner as oppressors and robbers; enemies of the state. They are subject to tax audits, antitrust prosecutions, investigations and shakedowns. Dissenters within these corporations cannot be tolerated; hence the firing of Damore and the purge which must inevitably take place if the company is going to continue feeding at the Government Trough.

In such a situation, all dissent must be (unscientifically) connected to racism, sexism and despotism. Compromise and obedience to "social" justice norms become the unifying principle – the dance to destruction begins.

When management is diverted from making the decisions that are in the best interest of the company (minus the left's "values"), the company begins leaking profits until the management can do nothing but fill out compliance forms and act to avoid moral outrage and shaming by government and media.

Once an executive is no longer allowed to speak his own mind, there is no hope that the company will be competitive. At this point, executives must hope there is someone around who can be bribed to look the other way. At this point, the only departments growing are the public relations and lobbying side of the business both of which rob the company of profits and make working at the company an utter drudgery. Group-think and group-speak are the new rules for survival among employees.

When the entire management of a company declares that it is open to new ideas, you can be sure they are not telling the truth. It is not possible for the management to be open to ideas when the only way they can keep their jobs is to do whatever the government tells them to do and they must pretend they believe in those "imposed" values from the bottom of their hearts. This is a telltale sign that this company is eventually going down.

These "forces" will ensure that the company is exposed to the competition that is itself greasing the wheels of government. When you consider that most large companies are beset by government bureaucrats from Labor, EEOC, Antitrust, IRS, FBI and DOJ, just to name a few (and not to mention all the foreign governments), you can be sure that the singular emotion of these people is not love for humanity but pure unadulterated fear. Every idea they espouse is intended, not to advance their personal values of diversity, inclusion, and love, but to please some bureaucrat and hope that he is not an envious monster who would destroy the company with a single decision of his own demented mind. That's why Mr. Damore was fired. His stream of consciousness argument about diversity didn't send the right signal to the people who want to eat Google for lunch.

Yet, there is an even more sinister and evil cause of all this; and that is our progressive educational system. Since they were children, most of these executives were indoctrinated in progressive schools. They were told they did not need to think, that the group was the sole repository of value in society, that thinking conceptually was not necessary and that the only important thing in the world is finding a group to love and to be part of. Collectivism was the highest value in their schools while gaining real knowledge was not as important as feeling loved by the group. When children hear this message every day in school as well as from parents, priests and college professors, their entire world is turned into a kindergarten where wishing makes it so and the most important thing to do is to smile, smile, smile. Don't be surprised, then, if they demand to be given privilege for their non-sexuality, their non-entity lives, their un-thinking minds and for their collective madness and gangsterism. They scream that they want to be loved for who they are, but they can't even tell you who they are. The one thing they know is that people should love them and if they don't, they should be fired as racists and haters.

In such an intellectual climate, it should not be surprising that today's corporations are run like children's kindergartens. Employees are coddled so they can find their place in the world; they are given blankets to lie on, time to meditate and plenty of games to play while each of them vies for the top position as the leader of their group. Ask them to do their best in the shortest amount of time and you are destroying their psychological happiness. They'd rather doodle and throw things. Don't make them cry. Criticizing their work to make them more productive would make them feel insecure. They can't deal with pressure like that. You might as well call it sexism and racism.

What the left has done to company's like Google is insist that they cease to be capitalist organizations seeking the most productive outcomes. Companies today must accept the false idea that capitalism has failed at providing an equitable society. This notion is sold to the nation as a scientific "finding" of the technocrats who believe that society can be "controlled" into prosperity. Notions about individualism and individual rights are considered passé and anyone ignorant enough to advocate such notions should be dismissed out of hand. Damore was right about the leftist echo chamber and he was right to suggest that the cause of Google's problem is diversity politics.

I've experienced this echo chamber when I worked in New York. There in the shadows of sky high buildings, I was told that I should shut up if I wanted to defend capitalism and individualism; that capitalism was not the solution to our economic problems and that government controls were the solution. I was not even allowed the opportunity to make an argument for my case. How can force create a better economy? No answer.

How can Google provide better services to its users when there is a person standing behind the management watching every step it makes; a person whose best argument is a gun sticking in their backs, a person telling them what the government thinks it should do to equalize men, women, blacks, whites, native Americans, etc., etc., etc. In such a situation, it wouldn't matter what Google did because the government could declare them guilty for doing anything.

The fact is, Google and other large companies in the clutches of government can only fail. This is because racism and genderism are not the problems they are made out to be. An argument can be made that all these divisions, white, black, brown, yellow, etc., are arbitrary and unscientific. There is only one race of humanity and that race is called humanity. Skin color, gender differences, or any other physical characteristics are not significant to any degree. They are not indicative of character, morality or intelligence.

And in a world where physical stamina is not always required for productive work, the world of people sitting at computers making decisions, the only characteristic they all share is their desire to be working at these jobs. In other words, when a government establishes arbitrary differences and creates arbitrary groups within a company, there is no chance that the company will be able to hire, promote and pay its employees according to merit. The government's gun is the destroyer of this company and the fearful, ineffectual management is riding a sinking ship.

But just who is the government protecting through the control it exerts over Google? Is it protecting women? Which women? The very few women who can't get a job because their skills don't match those needed by Google? Or the clear majority of individuals who have educated themselves for the very jobs that Google needs to fill?

How about the people of color who have never sat for hours at a computer learning about machine language, Boolean logic or even how to use a Word Processor? Is it Google's job to protect them? Or should it look for people who want to work according to higher standards? Will it be more competitive at achieving its mission of delivering the most relevant content to its customers if it creates positions that are not charged with achieving that mission?

In effect, the government is determining the rules of the game without regard to whether "protected" people can do the job. The only important thing is that "protected" groups are given preference over competent individuals who happen to belong to an unprotected group. If you value fairness, how is that fair?

We must ask ourselves an important question: What made Google a great company? Was it liberalism? Was it group-think? Was it diversity? It was none of these. What made Google great was the individual and his unfettered access to the knowledge needed to advance his life. Google was the best source for the world's knowledge and as such it helped countless individuals find better ideas, better jobs, better products and higher principles. Google served the individual, not the collective, not the gender, not the race. For Google, and for every corporation, its highest value is not the person of a particular color or gender; it is the individual of any color or gender. That is the value that is lost today at Google and at other large corporations. They have been diverted by government and collectivism from fulfilling their mission of serving the individual mind and providing him or her with the best knowledge.

Indeed, what does it mean for a VP of Diversity to proclaim his highest value to be diversity? What is his or her real value? It might surprise you to know that it isn't diversity – it is altruism, the sacrifice of the individual to the collective. Google must declare that its mission is not to provide a connection to the best knowledge but to sacrifice all other values to the "value" of sacrifice. It must declare to the world: "Don't hate us because we are successful. We really want to give it all away and we do it through every day and second that we breathe. We don't want money, we just want you to love us." How long will such a company provide the best search engine in the world? The enemy is at the gate, so they say.

Google was created by intelligent people with a mission to provide a service that no one else was providing. The values and services it returned to users enabled them to improve their lives. In a sense, Google elevated society because it elevated human knowledge and gave average people access to its benefits. But now, Google is not being run by those intelligent people. Instead men with guns have come in to tell Google what they need to do. Rather than give real value, they are instructed to be part of a social experiment whose goal is not to elevate the average man but to equalize all men; especially the intelligent people who must cater to the government's will. This isn't free society.

Google is not alone. Most likely, all major American corporations have been walking the tight rope of coercive government for decades. The individual is browbeaten by that social justice nonsense every day; but today they have been dragged into the arbitrariness of government by the universities and government contracts.

I remember, years ago, being dragged into the morass of diversity training at a major American corporation. I was the only minority in a room of other managers and you could cut the air with a knife. My company was hardly a bastion of racism and, for the most part, people advanced according to merit (as I had). You could tell that every manager in the room was angry that he was compelled to be in the "training" room and that he had to mouth all the platitudes about avoiding racism in the workplace. Oftentimes, I could feel the eyes of people in the room on me and I knew that not one of these managers thought he was part of a systemically racist system. Most felt wrongly accused and they were taking it out on me, because I too, like them, was forced to pretend that I agreed that our company had lots of racism in it. But it wasn't the accusation of racism that made them angry; it was the idea that they were forced to admit that they were racist. I think the company created lots of racism that day.

What happens when one individual sees through the government controls and decides to offer a reasoned argument against the unworkable diversity policies in place? Despite Mr. Damore's biological analysis, most of which is wrong, he does suggest a merit-based hiring system which would solve many of Google's problems. But he is apparently not cognizant of the role that government plays in all this. Although many in Google's management sincerely believe the altruistic notions of diversity and they have been thoroughly indoctrinated in it, the truth is that, even if they didn't believe in diversity, they would still be required to do all the things government demands. They must comply, or the government will cut off their government contracts and send many of them to anti-trust prison. Who wants to go to jail?

Can management conceive of a broad vision and then work to execute that vision? Not today at most American corporations. The government would have other ideas. What about developing long-range goals that must be accomplished over time by rational thought and action? No; what is rational thought and action? Such an idea does not exist in the world of the technocrat (the child of John Dewey). What about values that are derived from abstract concepts such as accomplishment, principles and universal truths? No; the Founding Fathers are passé. Can they work toward those values? No; they must work to accomplish only the immediate, the concrete – such as filling out government compliance forms, deciding on payoffs to government officials, campaign contributions, reading voluminous government regulations and ensuring that they have good relationships with their government representatives.

This is what "work" in a coercive society is made of; the concrete, the immediate, the compliant. Is it any wonder that our economy is being strangled to death and that available jobs go unfilled? Who wants to work in a corrupt environment like this? Everyone must be careful of everything he or she says and be constantly watching over his or her shoulder to see if anyone is listening; they must always be fearful of "whistle blowers" and of enemies eager to create scandal that will rob them of their jobs.

What is the ultimate cause of this madness, philosophically? It is cultural Marxism, the idea that capitalist institutions and corporations, are inherently exploitative and racist by nature. It is the class warfare fallacy. Under such an ideology, corporations must be tightly controlled by government to keep them from exploiting the classes (masses); and this is where society loses its capitalist merit-based nature. Under cultural Marxism, the individual is a pebble in the highway toward the vaunted utopia. One employee is no different from another. Each employee is a robot mindlessly doing what the corporation or government pays him to do, unimportant, expendable and common. Today, there are no individuals struggling for a better life, working harder than others, thinking harder than others, etc. Each must fit into a group and be exactly like (in every way) all other members of the group. Conformity has replaced production.

This even applies to the top executives of the corporations. According to the cultural Marxists, they are merely "lucky" tramps who have gotten a job among the elite of the company. The government considers them work horses and most of them feel that way about themselves. That's why they are so eager to be "democratic", kind, inclusive, people persons; and it is especially why so many of them plan on giving away their riches when they die (some even before they die); they have swallowed the notion that there is not a whit of difference between them and the homeless person with the paper cup on the street. And in this climate of government choosing winners and losers, they are right.

Government coercion is certainly an equalizer. Indeed, a coercive society such as ours can only divide people into tribes that have specific characteristics and goals. They come to work each day, unthinking and unmotivated; only with their tribal characteristics to guide them. They know they don't deserve their jobs, even though their jobs have been dumbed-down to hitting a key on a computer keyboard.

The machines have taken over. That's exactly what the government wants. Good bye, individualism. What our society needs is not the stultifying "progress" of coercive society, otherwise known as progressivism, but the clear, breathable air of freedom, individual rights and a limited government.

Robert George is a pseudonym for a retired former American business executive.